PAT SLOAN'S
Tantalizing Table Toppers

A Dozen Eye-Catching Quilts to Perk Up Your Home

Martingale®
Create with Confidence

Pat Sloan's Tantalizing Table Toppers:
A Dozen Eye-Catching Quilts to Perk Up Your Home
© 2022 by Pat Sloan

Martingale®
18939 120th Ave NE, Suite 101
Bothell, WA 98011-9511 USA
ShopMartingale.com

Printed in Hong Kong
27 26 25 24 23 22   8 7 6 5 4 3 2 1

Library of Congress Cataloging-in-Publication Data is available upon request.

ISBN: 978-1-68356-179-8

MISSION STATEMENT

We empower makers who use fabric and yarn
to make life more enjoyable.

CREDITS

**PUBLISHER AND
CHIEF VISIONARY OFFICER**
Jennifer Erbe Keltner

CONTENT DIRECTOR
Karen Costello Soltys

DESIGN MANAGER
Adrienne Smitke

TECHNICAL EDITOR
Nancy Mahoney

PRODUCTION MANAGER
Regina Girard

COPY EDITOR
Sheila Chapman Ryan

PHOTOGRAPHERS
Adam Albright
Brent Kane

ILLUSTRATOR
Sandy Loi

SPECIAL THANKS
*Some of the photography for this book was taken at
the home of Julie Smiley in Des Moines, Iowa.*

Contents

Introduction 5

    Italian Café 7

    Life's a Picnic 11

    Flower Stand 21

    Main Street Perks 27

    Game Night 31

    Tea Time 39

    Family Gathering 43

    Winter Bliss 51

    French Bistro 59

    U-Pick 63

    Breakfast Club 69

    Summer Fun 75

Acknowledgments 80

About the Author 80

Introduction

Hello, my friends!

One of life's greatest pleasures is meeting with good friends and family for a visit—and to share yummy cookies, delicious cakes, and wonderful things to drink. The visit might be in our homes or we might go out somewhere for a relaxing chat. Come along with me as we travel to different cozy places and enjoy various delicious treats.

As quilters we love to create coziness by decorating with table runners and toppers. We make them for ourselves and we give them as gifts. They're the perfect size to make quickly, and they set the stage for a splendid time. Decorating our tables creates the mood, celebrates each season, and adds a little sparkle to any event.

I'd love to meet you for a cake and coffee, but until then, join my quilting community on Facebook, Quilt Along with Pat Sloan. And if you love baking and cooking, you're also invited to join my other Facebook community, Kitchen Adventures with Pat Sloan. We share what we're making, talk about what worked or didn't, and support each other when trying new recipes.

Every gathering is special when you have something yummy to eat. I want to leave you with the first recipe my mother-in-law, Madge, gave me. You'll find her Apple Cake recipe on page 49. I love you and I'll see you online!

~Pat

Italian Café

Italian cafés do coffee like none other. I'm inspired by the Italian traditions around "having a coffee." Italians enjoy small, strong cups of coffee during the day at the café—no to-go orders. Why not create the relaxing feel of an Italian café in your kitchen with blocks that mimic fine Italian tile work in bold colors?

FINISHED TABLE RUNNER: 17½" × 35½" | FINISHED BLOCK: 6" × 6"

MATERIALS

Yardage is based on 42"-wide fabric. Fat eighths measure 9" × 21".

- ⅓ yard of cream print for blocks and inner border
- ⅞ yard of red print for blocks, outer border, and binding
- ⅓ yard of white with green floral for blocks
- ¼ yard of orange print for blocks
- 1 fat eighth of green print for blocks
- 1⅛ yards of fabric for backing
- 22" × 40" piece of batting

CUTTING

All measurements include ¼" seam allowances.

From the cream print, cut:
1 strip, 2½" × 42"; crosscut into 10 squares, 2½" × 2½"
2 strips, 2" × 42"; crosscut into 20 pieces, 2" × 3½"
3 strips, 1" × 42"; crosscut into:
    2 strips, 1" × 31½"
    2 strips, 1" × 12½"

From the red print, cut:
4 strips, 2½" × 42"; crosscut into:
    2 strips, 2½" × 35½"
    2 strips, 2½" × 13½"
    10 squares, 2½" × 2½"
3 strips, 2" × 42"; crosscut into 60 squares, 2" × 2"
3 strips, 2¼" × 42"

From the white with green floral, cut:
1 strip, 2½" × 42"; crosscut into 10 squares, 2½" × 2½"
2 strips, 2" × 42"; crosscut into 40 squares, 2" × 2"

From the orange print, cut:
1 strip, 2½" × 42"; crosscut into 10 squares, 2½" × 2½"
2 strips, 2" × 42"; crosscut into 20 pieces, 2" × 3½"

From the green print, cut:
2 strips, 2" × 21"; crosscut into 20 squares, 2" × 2"

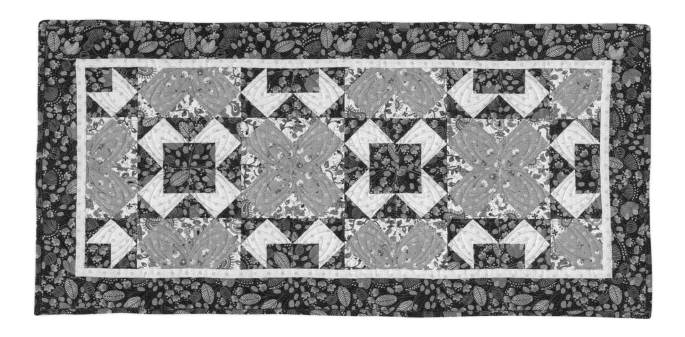

MAKING THE BLOCKS

Press all seam allowances in the direction indicated by the arrows.

1 Draw a diagonal line from corner to corner on the wrong side of the cream print 2½" squares. Place a marked square right sides together with a red 2½" square. Sew ¼" from both sides of the drawn line. Cut the unit apart on the marked line to make two half-square-triangle units. Make 20 red/cream units and trim them to measure 2" square, including seam allowances.

Make 20 units.

2 Draw a diagonal line from corner to corner on the wrong side of the white with green floral 2½" squares. Repeat step 1, using the marked squares and the orange 2½" squares to make 20 orange/green floral units. Trim the units to measure 2" square, including seam allowances.

Make 20 units.

3 Draw a diagonal line from corner to corner on the wrong side of 40 red 2" squares. Place a marked square on one end of a cream print 2" × 3½" piece, right sides together. Sew on the marked line. Trim the excess corner fabric ¼" from the stitched line. Place a marked square on the opposite end of the cream piece. Sew and trim as before to make a flying-geese unit measuring 2" × 3½", including seam allowances. Make 20 red units.

Make 20 units,
2" × 3½".

4 Draw a diagonal line from corner to corner on the wrong side of the white with green floral 2" squares. Repeat step 3 using the marked squares and the orange 2" × 3½" pieces to make 20 orange flying-geese units measuring 2" × 3½", including seam allowances.

Make 20 units,
2" × 3½".

5 Lay out one red 2" square, one red/cream triangle unit from step 1, and one red flying-geese unit. Join the square and triangle unit. Add the flying-geese unit to make a unit measuring 3½" square, including seam allowances. Make 20 A units.

Make 20 A units,
3½" × 3½".

6 Lay out one green square, one orange/green floral triangle unit from step 2, and one orange flying-geese unit. Join the square and triangle unit. Add the flying-geese unit to make a unit measuring 3½" square, including seam allowances. Make 20 B units.

Make 20 B units,
3½" × 3½".

7 Lay out two A and two B units, rotating the units as shown. Sew the units into rows. Join the rows to make a block measuring 6½" square, including seam allowances. Make 10 blocks.

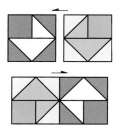 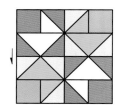

Make 10 blocks,
6½" × 6½".

ASSEMBLING THE TABLE RUNNER

1 Lay out the blocks in two rows of five blocks each, rotating them as shown in the table-runner assembly diagram below. Sew the blocks into rows. Join the rows to make the runner center, which should measure 12½" × 30½", including seam allowances.

2 Sew the cream print 1" × 12½" strips to the short ends of the runner. Sew the cream print 1" × 31½" strips to the long edges. The table runner should measure 13½" × 31½", including seam allowances.

3 Sew the red 2½" × 13½" strips to the short ends of the runner. Sew the red 2½" × 35½" strips to the long edges. The table runner should measure 17½" × 35½".

FINISHING THE TABLE RUNNER

For more details on any finishing steps, visit ShopMartingale.com/HowtoQuilt for free downloadable information.

1 Layer the runner top with batting and backing; baste the layers together.

2 Quilt by hand or machine. The table runner shown is machine quilted with curved lines and feather plumes in the blocks. A feather design is stitched in the outer border.

3 Use the red 2¼"-wide strips to make double-fold binding. Attach the binding to the table runner.

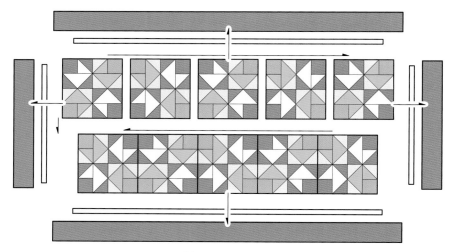

Table-runner assembly

Life's a Picnic

I adore picnics. Picnic foods equal fun to me. My favorites are potato salad, burgers, hot dogs, and deli sandwiches wrapped in waxed paper. The big finish? S'mores, of course! But don't wait for the weather to be just right. Gear up for an indoor picnic any day and set the scene with a summery table topper as the star, before the stars in the night sky come out!

FINISHED TABLE TOPPER: 48½" × 48½" | FINISHED BLOCK: 12" × 12"

MATERIALS

Yardage is based on 42"-wide fabric.

- 1⅝ yards of light A print for blocks, sashing, and inner border
- ¼ yard *each* of peach and green gingham for blocks
- ¾ yard of gray floral for blocks
- 5 pieces, 6" × 10", of peach prints for blocks
- 4 pieces, 6" × 10", of green prints for blocks
- 2 pieces, 6" × 8", of light B prints for blocks
- ⅝ yard of peach stripe for sashing and binding
- 23 squares, 6" × 6", of assorted prints for outer border
- 3⅛ yards of fabric for backing
- 55" × 55" piece of batting

CUTTING

All measurements include ¼" seam allowances.

From the light A print, cut:
2 strips, 4" × 42"; crosscut into 18 squares, 4" × 4"
6 strips, 3½" × 42"; crosscut into 36 pieces, 3½" × 6½"
9 strips, 2½" × 42"; crosscut 4 of the strips into 12 strips, 2½" × 12½"

From the peach gingham, cut:
10 squares, 4" × 4"

From the green gingham, cut:
8 squares, 4" × 4"

From the gray floral, cut:
7 strips, 3½" × 42"; crosscut into 72 squares, 3½" × 3½"

From *each* of the peach prints, cut:
2 strips, 2½" × 6½" (10 total)
2 squares, 2½" × 2½" (10 total)

From *each* of the green prints, cut:
2 strips, 2½" × 6½" (8 total)
2 squares, 2½" × 2½" (8 total)

Continued on page 13

Continued from page 11

From *each* of the light B prints, cut:

5 squares, 2½" × 2½" (10 total; 1 is extra)

From the peach stripe, cut:

2 strips, 2½" × 42"; crosscut into 20 squares,
   2½" × 2½"
6 strips, 2¼" × 42"

From *each* of the assorted print squares, cut:

4 squares, 2½" × 2½" (92 total)

MAKING THE BLOCKS

Press all seam allowances in the direction indicated
by the arrows.

1 Draw a diagonal line from corner to corner on
the wrong side of each light A 4" square. Place
a marked square right sides together with a peach
gingham square. Sew ¼" from both sides of the
drawn line. Cut the unit apart on the marked line
to make two half-square-triangle units. Make 20
peach units and trim them to measure 3½" square,
including seam allowances.

Make 20 units.

2 Repeat step 1 using the remaining marked
squares and the green gingham squares to
make 16 green units. Trim the units to measure
3½" square, including seam allowances.

Make 16 units.

3 Draw a diagonal line from corner to corner on
the wrong side of the gray squares. Place a
marked square on one end of a light A 3½" × 6½"

piece, right sides together. Sew on the marked line.
Trim the excess corner fabric ¼" from the stitched
line. Place a marked square on the opposite end of
the light piece. Sew and trim as before to make a
flying-geese unit measuring 3½" × 6½", including
seam allowances. Make 36 units. (If desired, set
aside the trimmed triangles to make the place mats
on page 18.)

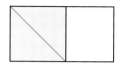 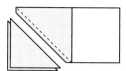

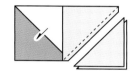 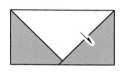

Make 36 units,
3½" × 6½".

4 Lay out two peach print 2½" × 6½" strips,
two peach print squares, and one light B
square as shown. The peach print should be the
same throughout. Sew the squares into rows. Join
the rows to make a center unit measuring 6½"
square, including seam allowances. Make five peach
units. In the same way, make four green center units
using the green print strips and squares and the
remaining light B squares.

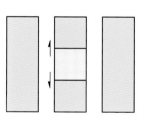 

Make 5 units,
6½" × 6½".

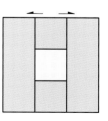

Make 4 units,
6½" × 6½".

5 Lay out four peach half-square-triangle units, four flying-geese units, and one peach center unit. Sew the units into rows. Join the rows to make a peach block measuring 12½" square, including seam allowances. Make five blocks.

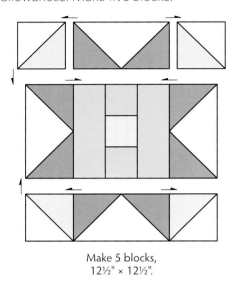

Make 5 blocks,
12½" × 12½".

6 Lay out four green half-square-triangle units, four flying-geese units, and one green center unit. Sew the units into rows. Join the rows to make a green block measuring 12½" square, including seam allowances. Make four blocks.

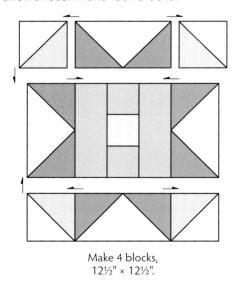

Make 4 blocks,
12½" × 12½".

ASSEMBLING THE TABLE TOPPER

Refer to the table-topper assembly diagram on page 16 as needed.

1 Draw a diagonal line from corner to corner on the wrong side of 16 peach stripe squares. Sew a marked square to one end of a light A 2½" × 12½" strip, making sure to orient the marked line as shown. Make eight side sashing units measuring 2½" × 12½", including seam allowances.

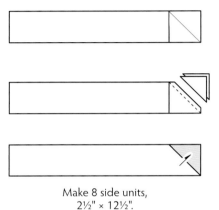

Make 8 side units,
2½" × 12½".

2 Sew marked squares on both ends of a light A 2½" × 12½" strip, making sure to orient the marked lines as shown. Make four center sashing units measuring 2½" × 12½", including seam allowances.

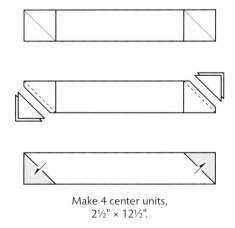

Make 4 center units,
2½" × 12½".

3 Join two peach blocks, one green block, and two side sashing units to make the top block row. Repeat to make the bottom block row. The rows should measure 12½" × 40½", including seam allowances.

4 Join two green blocks, one peach block, and two center sashing units to make the center block row. The row should measure 12½" × 40½", including seam allowances.

5 Join two side sashing units, two peach stripe squares, and one center sashing unit to make a sashing row measuring 2½" × 40½", including seam allowances. Make two rows.

6 Lay out the block rows and sashing rows, alternating their positions. Join the rows to make the topper center, which should measure 40½" square, including seam allowances.

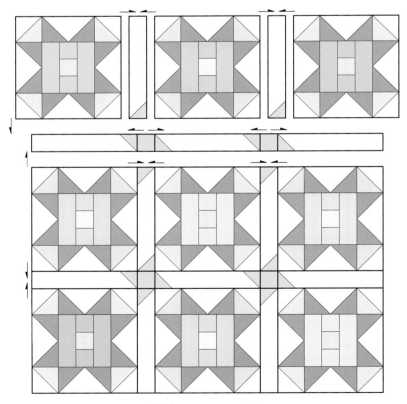

Table-topper assembly

ADDING THE BORDERS

1 Join the remaining light A 2½"-wide strips end to end. From the pieced strip, cut two 44½"-long strips and two 40½"-long strips. Sew the shorter strips to the top and bottom edges of the topper center. Sew the longer strips to the left and right sides as shown below. The topper should measure 44½" square, including seam allowances.

2 Join 22 assorted 2½" squares to make a top border measuring 2½" × 44½", including seam allowances. Repeat to make the bottom border. Join 24 assorted print squares to make a side border measuring 2½" × 48½", including seam allowances. Make two side borders.

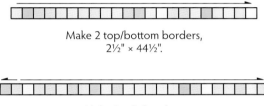

Make 2 top/bottom borders,
2½" × 44½".

Make 2 side borders,
2½" × 48½".

3 Sew the borders to the top and bottom of the table topper and then to the left and right sides. The quilt top should measure 48½" square.

FINISHING THE TABLE TOPPER

For more details on any finishing steps, visit ShopMartingale.com/HowtoQuilt for free downloadable information.

1 Layer the table-topper top with batting and backing; baste the layers together.

2 Quilt by hand or machine. The topper shown is machine quilted with an allover pattern of swirls and flowers.

3 Use the peach stripe 2¼"-wide strips to make double-fold binding. Attach the binding to the table topper.

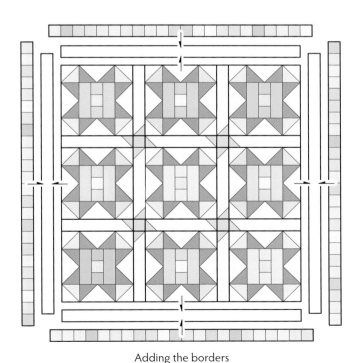

Adding the borders

Place Mats

FINISHED PLACE MAT: 18½" × 14½"

Add a little sunshine
to your table with
a pair of perky
place mats. Treating
them with fabric
protectant will
extend their use.

MATERIALS

Yardage is based on 42"-wide fabric. Yields 2 place mats.

- 2 pieces, 9" × 18½", of white floral for center section
- 2 strips, 1¼" × 18½", of peach print for inner border
- 2 strips, 1¼" × 18½", of green print for inner border
- 18 squares, 3" × 3", of light print for outer border*
- 18 squares, 3" × 3", of gray print for outer border*
- 2 strips, 2¼" × 42", of peach print for binding
- 2 strips, 2¼" × 24", of green print for binding
- 2 pieces, 16" × 20", for place-mat back
- 2 pieces, 16" × 20", of batting

Instead of cutting squares, you can use the 36 light and 36 gray triangles left over from making the flying-geese units for the table topper (see page 13).

MAKING THE PLACE MATS

Instructions are for making the peach place mat. Repeat to make the green place mat. Press all seam allowances in the direction indicated by the arrows.

1 Draw a diagonal line from corner to corner on the wrong side of nine light 3" squares. Place a marked square right sides together with a gray square. Sew ¼" from both sides of the drawn line. Cut the unit apart on the marked line to make two half-square-triangle units. Make 18 units and trim them to measure 2½" square, including seam allowances.

2½"

2½"

Make 18 units.

2 Join nine half-square-triangle units to make a strip measuring 2½" × 18½", including seam allowances. Press the seam allowances open. Make two strips.

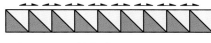

Make 2 strips, 2½" × 18½".

3 Sew the peach 1¼" × 18½" strips to the long edges of a white floral piece. Sew a triangle strip from step 2 to the top and bottom edges to make the place-mat front. The place mat should measure 18½" × 14½".

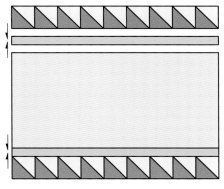

Place-mat assembly

4 Layer the place mat top with batting and backing; baste the layers together.

5 Machine quilt swirls in the center section and curved lines in the triangles.

6 Use the peach 2¼"-wide strips to make double-fold binding. Attach the binding to the place mat.

Flower Stand

A farmers market in St. Petersburg, Florida, is on the water and filled with amazing goodies. My family shopped for cheese, salsa, pasta, and gorgeous flowers! Next to people-watching at the market, lingering at a flower stand is my favorite way to pass the time. The colors and variety inspired me to meld floral fabrics and patchwork flowers for a lasting memory.

FINISHED TABLE RUNNER: 18½" × 44½" | FINISHED BLOCK: 12" × 12"

MATERIALS

Yardage is based on 42"-wide fabric. Fat eighths measure 9" × 21".

- ½ yard of red linen for blocks and binding
- ¼ yard of red dot for blocks and outer border
- 3 fat eighths of assorted red prints for blocks
- 1 fat eighth of yellow linen for blocks
- 4 fat eighths of assorted yellow prints for blocks
- ⅓ yard of blue print for blocks and sashing
- ¼ yard of black print for blocks
- ¼ yard of blue linen for inner border
- ¼ yard of blue floral for outer border
- 1⅜ yards of fabric for backing
- 23" × 49" piece of batting

CUTTING

All measurements include ¼" seam allowances.

From the red linen, cut:
1 strip, 4" × 42"; crosscut into 8 squares, 4" × 4"
4 strips, 2¼" × 42"

From the red dot, cut:
5 squares, 4" × 4"
8 squares, 2½" × 2½"

From the red print fat eighths, cut a *total* of:
19 squares, 4" × 4"

From the yellow linen, cut:
4 squares, 4" × 4"

From *1* yellow print, cut:
3 squares, 4" × 4"
8 squares, 2½" × 2½"

From the remaining yellow prints, cut a *total* of:
9 squares, 4" × 4"

From the blue print, cut:
3 strips, 2½" × 42"; crosscut into 36 squares, 2½" × 2½"
1 strip, 1½" × 42"; crosscut into 2 strips, 1½" × 12½"

Continued on page 22

Continued from page 21

From the black print, cut:

2 strips, 3½" × 42"; crosscut into 12 squares,
  3½" × 3½"

From the blue linen, cut:

3 strips, 1½" × 42"; crosscut *1 of the strips* into
  2 strips, 1½" × 12½"

From the blue floral, cut:

3 strips, 2½" × 42"; crosscut *1 of the strips* into
  2 strips, 2½" × 14½"

MAKING THE BLOCKS

Press all seam allowances as shown by the arrows.

1 Draw a diagonal line from corner to corner on the wrong side of 16 of the red print, red linen, and red dot 4" squares. Place a marked square right sides together with a different red square. Sew ¼" from both sides of the drawn line. Cut the unit apart on the marked line to make two half-square-triangle units. Make 32 red units and trim them to measure 3½" square, including seam allowances.

Make 32 units.

2 Draw a diagonal line from corner to corner on the wrong side of eight of the yellow linen and yellow print 4" squares. Repeat step 1, using the marked squares and the remaining yellow 4" squares to make 16 yellow units. Trim the units to measure 3½" square, including seam allowances.

Make 16 units.

3 Draw a diagonal line from corner to corner on the wrong side of the blue print 2½" squares. Place a marked square on one corner of a red triangle unit, right sides together, noting the orientation of the unit and the marked line. Sew on the marked line. Trim the excess corner fabric ¼" from the stitched line. Make 24 red units measuring 3½" square, including seam allowances.

Make 24 units,
3½" × 3½".

4 Repeat step 3 using the remaining marked blue squares and the yellow triangle units to make 12 units measuring 3½" square, including seam allowances.

Make 12 units,
3½" × 3½".

5 Draw a diagonal line from corner to corner on the wrong side of the black squares. Place a marked square on top of a red triangle unit, making sure the marked line is perpendicular to the seamline. Sew on the marked line. Trim the excess corner fabric ¼" from the stitched line. Make eight red units measuring 3½" square, including seam allowances. Repeat to make four yellow units using the remaining marked black squares and yellow triangle units.

Make 8 units,   Make 4 units,
3½" × 3½".   3½" × 3½".

6 Draw a diagonal line from corner to corner on the wrong side of eight yellow print and four red dot 2½" squares. Place a marked yellow square on the black corner of a red unit from step 5. Sew on the marked line. Trim the excess corner fabric ¼" from the stitched line. Make eight red center units measuring 3½" square, including seam allowances. Repeat to make four yellow center units using the marked red squares and yellow triangle units.

7 Lay out 12 red units from step 3 and four red center units from step 6, rotating the units as shown. Sew the units into rows. Join the rows to make a block measuring 12½" square, including seam allowances. Make two blocks.

Make 8 center units,   Make 4 center units,
3½" × 3½".   3½" × 3½".

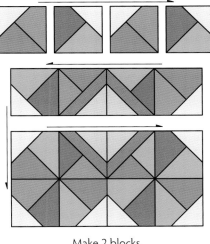

Make 2 blocks,
12½" × 12½".

8 Lay out the yellow units from step 4 and the yellow center units from step 6, rotating the units as shown. Sew the units into rows. Join the rows to make a block measuring 12½" square, including seam allowances.

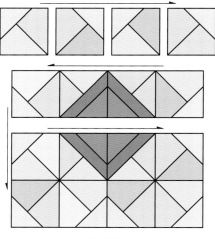

Make 1 block,
12½" × 12½".

ASSEMBLING THE TABLE RUNNER

1 Lay out the two red blocks, one yellow block, and two blue print strips, alternating their positions as shown in the table-runner assembly diagram on page 25. Join the blocks and strips to make a row measuring 12½" × 38½", including seam allowances.

2 Sew the blue linen 1½" × 12½" strips to the short ends of the table runner. Join the remaining blue linen 1½"-wide strips end to end. From the pieced strip, cut two 40½"-long strips and sew them to the long edges. The table runner should measure 14½" × 40½", including seam allowances.

3 Sew the blue floral 2½" × 14½" strips to the short ends of the table runner. Join the remaining blue floral 2½"-wide strips end to end. From the pieced strip, cut two 40½"-long strips. Sew a red dot 2½" square to each end of both strips and then sew the strips to the long edges of the runner. The table runner should measure 18½" × 44½".

Always in Season

The beauty of stitching up your own everlasting flowers is that you can match them to a variety of items to suit your needs—the room colors, a set of dishes, a season (can you see pansies or poinsettias?), or a favorite piece of artwork near your tabletop. Make several to swap out for the seasons!

FINISHING THE TABLE RUNNER

For more details on any finishing steps, visit ShopMartingale.com/HowtoQuilt for free downloadable information.

1 Layer the runner top with batting and backing; baste the layers together.

2 Quilt by hand or machine. The table runner shown is machine quilted with curved lines in the blocks. Bubbles are stitched in the inner border and sashing. A swirl motif is stitched in the outer border.

3 Use the red linen 2¼"-wide strips to make double-fold binding. Attach the binding to the table runner.

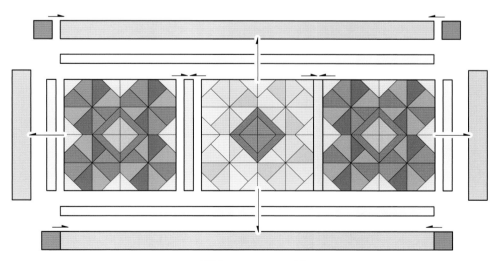

Table-runner assembly

Main Street Perks

My dream would be to own a darling little coffee shop in a walkable neighborhood. I'd have comfy chairs, cozy tables, and, of course, quilted table runners. We'd serve light lunches, little noshes, irresistible desserts, and relaxing beverages. It'd be the perfect spot for friends to meet. I love to make table runners so I can set the mood to suit my dreams!

FINISHED TABLE RUNNER: 16¼" × 45½"

MATERIALS

Yardage is based on 42"-wide fabric.

- ¾ yard *total* of assorted red and blue prints for braid
- ⅝ yard of navy floral for border and binding
- 1½ yards of fabric for backing
- 23" × 52" piece of batting

CUTTING

All measurements include ¼" seam allowances.

From the assorted prints, cut a *total* of:
35 strips, 2½" × 10"

From the navy floral, cut:
4 strips, 2½" × 42"; crosscut *1 of the strips* into
    2 strips, 2½" × 16¼"
4 strips, 2¼" × 42"

ASSEMBLING THE TABLE RUNNER

Press seam allowances in the directions indicated by the arrows.

1   Join two different print strips along their long edges. Press and sew a different print strip to the top edge.

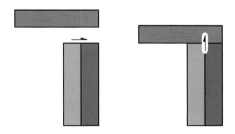

2   Sew print strips to the right and top edges of the unit from step 1.

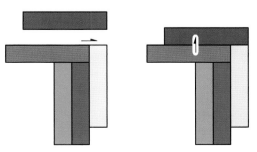

3 Continue sewing strips to the right and then top edges until you have used all 35 print strips. Press all seam allowances toward each newly added strip.

of the braid. Trim the bottom edge in the same way. Measure 41½" from the trimmed bottom edge and trim the top edge. The braid should measure 12¼" × 41½", including seam allowances.

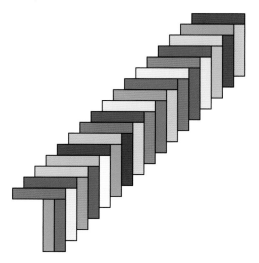

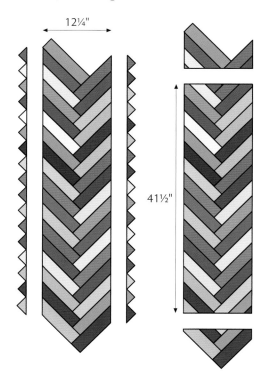

4 On one long side of the braid, align a ruler with the inside point of the seam intersection, placing the ruler's 45° line on a seamline. Trim along the edge of the ruler, moving the ruler along the length of the braid. Repeat to trim the other side

5 Join the three navy 2½" × 42" strips end to end. From the pieced strip, cut two 41½"-long strips. Sew the strips to the long edges of the braid. Sew the navy 2½" × 16¼" strips to the ends of the runner. The table runner should measure 16¼" × 45½".

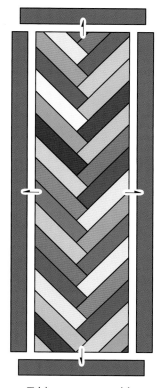

Table-runner assembly

FINISHING THE TABLE RUNNER

For more details on any finishing steps, visit ShopMartingale.com/HowtoQuilt for free downloadable information.

1 Layer the runner top with batting and backing; baste the layers together.

2 Quilt by hand or machine. The table runner shown is machine quilted with a leaf and vine design in each of the strips and in the border.

3 Use the navy 2¼"-wide strips to make double-fold binding. Attach the binding to the table runner.

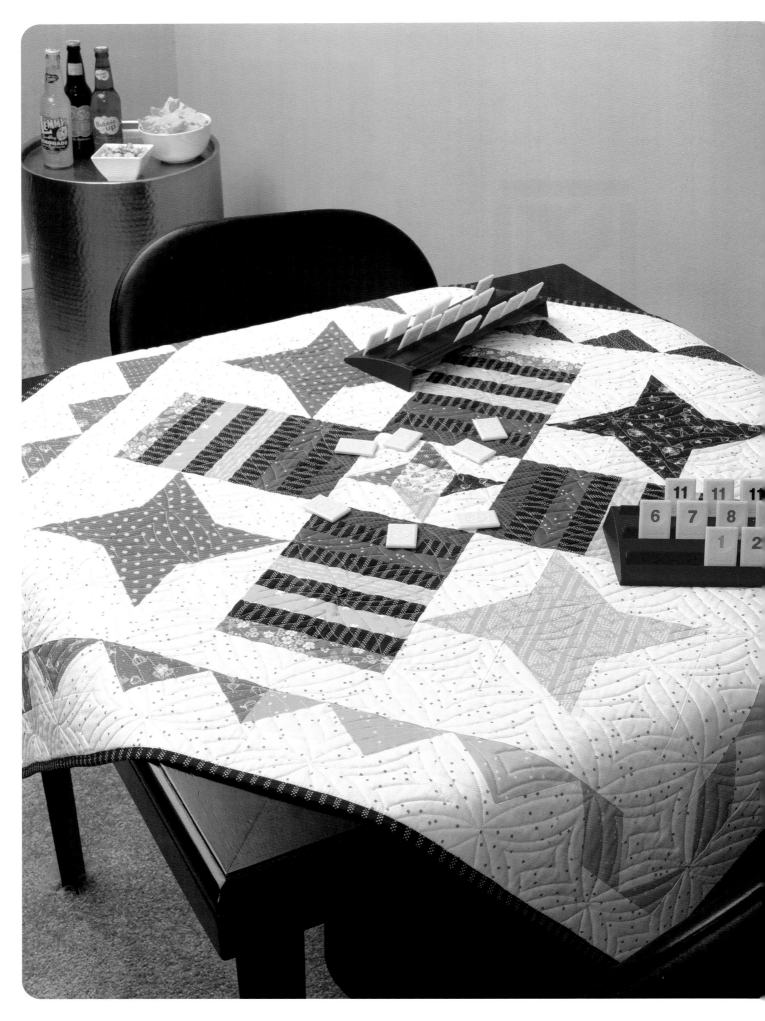

Game Night

Do you have a family game night? I love to get together with friends and family to play cards, board games, or video games. As a kid, my games of choice were Life and Candy Land. Break out the chips, pop some popcorn, and whip up a "Game Night" table topper in colors that correspond to your family's favorite games to set the mood for fun for everyone!

FINISHED TOPPER: 36½" × 36½" | FINISHED STAR BLOCK: 9" × 9"

MATERIALS

Yardage is based on 42"-wide fabric. Fat eighths measure 9" × 21". Label each of your fat eighths as indicated below for easier cutting.

- 1⅓ yards of white print for blocks and borders
- 3 fat eighths of assorted red prints (A–C) for blocks and ribbon border
- 4 fat eighths of assorted green prints (A–D) for blocks and ribbon border
- 4 fat eighths of assorted yellow prints (A–D) for blocks and ribbon border
- 2 fat eighths of navy prints (A and B) for blocks and ribbon border
- ½ yard of navy stripe for blocks and binding
- 1 square, 2½" × 2½", of white floral for Center Star block
- 2⅓ yards of fabric for backing*
- 41" × 41" piece of batting

*If the backing fabric is at least 42" wide, you can use a single width of 1¼ yards.

CUTTING

As you cut the red, green, yellow, and navy prints, keep like fabrics together. All measurements include ¼" seam allowances.

From the white print, cut:
1 strip, 4" × 42"; crosscut into 8 squares, 4" × 4"
2 strips, 3½" × 42"; crosscut into 16 squares, 3½" × 3½"
1 strip, 3" × 42"; crosscut into 10 squares, 3" × 3". Cut *2 of the squares* in half diagonally to yield 4 triangles.
11 strips, 2½" × 42"; crosscut into:
    2 strips, 2½" × 36½"
    2 strips, 2½" × 32½"
    2 strips, 2½" × 28½"
    2 strips, 2½" × 24½"
    52 squares, 2½" × 2½"

From *each* of the red, green, yellow, and navy A prints, cut:
2 squares, 4" × 4" (8 total)
1 square, 3½" × 3½" (4 total)
1 square, 3" × 3"; cut in half diagonally to yield 2 triangles (8 total; 1 triangle of each color is extra)

Continued on page 32

Continued from page 31

From *each* of the red B, green B, green C, yellow B, and yellow C prints, cut:

4 strips, 1½" × 6½" (20 total)

From *each* of the red C, green D, yellow D, and navy B prints, cut:

6 pieces, 2½" × 4½" (24 total)

2 squares, 3" × 3" (8 total)

From the navy stripe, cut:

3 strips, 1½" × 42"; crosscut into 16 strips, 1½" × 6½"

4 strips, 2¼" × 42"

MAKING THE LARGE STAR BLOCKS

Press all seam allowances in the direction indicated by the arrows.

1 Draw a diagonal line from corner to corner on the wrong side of the white 4" squares. Place a marked square right sides together with a red A 4" square. Sew ¼" from both sides of the drawn line. Cut the unit apart on the marked line to make two half-square-triangle units. Make four units and trim them to measure 3½" square, including seam allowances. Repeat using the marked squares and green A, yellow A, and navy A 4" squares to make four units of each color.

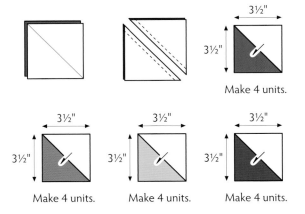

Make 4 units.

Make 4 units. Make 4 units. Make 4 units.

2 Lay out four white 3½" squares, four red half-square-triangle units, and one red A 3½" square. Sew the squares and units into rows. Join the rows to make a red Large Star block measuring 9½" square, including seam allowances. Repeat to make one green, one yellow, and one navy Large Star block.

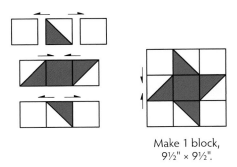

Make 1 block, 9½" × 9½".

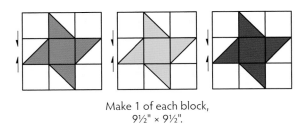

Make 1 of each block, 9½" × 9½".

MAKING THE CENTER STAR BLOCK

1 Sew a white triangle to the long edge of a red A triangle to make a half-square-triangle unit. Trim the unit to measure 2½" square, including seam allowances. Repeat using the green A, yellow A, and navy A triangles to make one unit of each color.

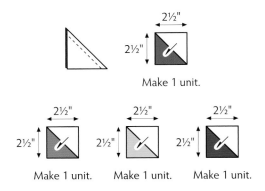

Make 1 unit.

Make 1 unit. Make 1 unit. Make 1 unit.

2 Lay out four white print 2½" squares, the half-square-triangle units from step 1, and the white floral 2½" square. Sew the squares and units into rows. Join the rows to make a Center Star block measuring 6½" square, including seam allowances.

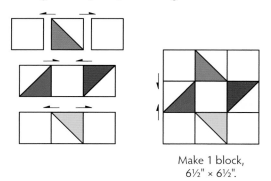

Make 1 block,
6½" × 6½".

MAKING THE PATHWAY BLOCKS

Join one red B, one yellow B, one yellow C, one green B, one green C, and four navy stripe 1½" × 6½" strips, alternating their positions, to make a block. Make four blocks measuring 6½" × 9½", including seam allowances.

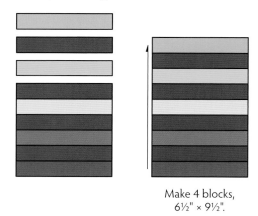

Make 4 blocks,
6½" × 9½".

ASSEMBLING THE TABLE TOPPER

Referring to the table-topper assembly diagram above right, lay out the Large Star blocks, Pathway blocks, and Center Star block in three rows of three blocks each. Sew the blocks into rows. Join the rows

to make the topper center, which should measure 24½" square, including seam allowances.

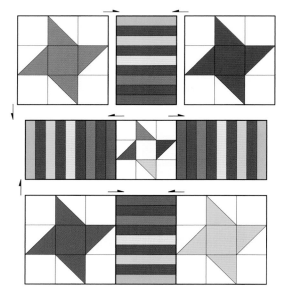

Table-topper assembly

MAKING THE RIBBON BORDER

1 Mark a diagonal line from corner to corner on the wrong side of the white print 2½" squares.

2 Place a marked square on one end of a red C piece, right sides together. Sew on the marked line. Trim the excess corner fabric ¼" from the stitched line. Place a marked square on the opposite end of the red piece. Sew and trim as before to make a flying-geese unit measuring 2½" × 4½", including seam allowances. Make four red units.

Make 4 units,
2½" × 4½".

3 Repeat step 2 using the marked white squares and the green D, yellow D, and navy B pieces. Make four units of each color.

Make 4 of each unit,
2½" × 4½".

4 Place a marked white square on one end of a red C piece, right sides together. Sew on the marked line. Trim the excess corner fabric ¼" from the stitched line. Place a marked square on the opposite end of the red piece, noting the direction of the marked line. Sew and trim as before to make an end unit measuring 2½" × 4½", including seam allowances. Make one unit. Repeat to make one reversed unit, making sure to reverse the orientation of the marked lines.

Make 1 unit and 1 reversed unit,
2½" × 4½".

This Way and That

When you're in the zone making many units, it's easy to forget to refer back to the instructions, especially regarding pressing. The arrows on the illustrations indicate the direction to press your seam allowances to help you more easily join pieces later as seam allowances will nest together.

---

5 Repeat step 4 using the remaining marked white squares and the green D, yellow D, and navy B pieces. Make one unit and one reversed unit of each color.

Make 1 unit and 1 reversed unit,
2½" × 4½".

Make 1 unit and 1 reversed unit,
2½" × 4½".

Make 1 unit and 1 reversed unit,
2½" × 4½".

6 Draw a diagonal line from corner to corner on the wrong side of each remaining white print 3" square. Place a marked square right sides together with a red C square. Sew ¼" from both sides of the drawn line. Cut the unit apart on the marked line to make two half-square-triangle units. Make four units and trim them to measure 2½" square, including seam allowances. Repeat using the green D, yellow D, and navy B squares to make four units of each color. (One unit from each color will be extra.)

Make 4 units.

Make 4 units.　Make 4 units.　Make 4 units.

7 To make the left side border, join one red end unit, two red flying-geese units, one red triangle unit, one green triangle unit, two green flying-geese units, and one green reversed end unit. To make the right side border, join one navy end unit, two navy flying-geese units, one navy triangle unit, one yellow triangle unit, two yellow flying-geese units, and one yellow reversed end unit. The borders should measure 2½" × 28½", including seam allowances.

Make 1 left side border,
2½" × 28½".

Make 1 right side border,
2½" × 28½".

8 To make the top border, join two green triangle units, one green end unit, two green flying-geese units, two navy triangle units, two navy flying-geese units, and one navy reversed end unit. To make the bottom border, join two yellow triangle units, one yellow end unit, two yellow flying-geese units, two red triangle units, two red flying-geese units, and one red reversed end unit. The borders should measure 2½" × 32½", including seam allowances.

Make 1 top border,
2½" × 32½".

Make 1 bottom border,
2½" × 32½".

ADDING THE BORDERS

1 Sew the white print 2½" × 24½" strips to the left and right sides of the topper center. Sew the white print 2½" × 28½" strips to the top and bottom edges. The topper should measure 28½" square, including seam allowances.

2 Sew the ribbon borders to the left and right sides and then the top and bottom edges of the topper. The topper should measure 32½" square, including seam allowances.

3 Sew the white print 2½" × 32½" strips to the left and right sides of the topper. Sew the white print 2½" × 36½" strips to the top and bottom edges. The topper should measure 36½" square.

FINISHING THE TABLE TOPPER

For more details on any finishing steps, visit ShopMartingale.com/HowtoQuilt for free downloadable information.

1 Layer the quilt top with batting and backing; baste the layers together.

2 Quilt by hand or machine. The table topper shown is machine quilted with an allover design of interlocking curved lines.

3 Use the navy stripe 2¼"-wide strips to make double-fold binding. Attach the binding to the table topper.

Adding the borders

Tea Time

I grew up on tea: hot tea, iced tea, and flavored tea. I have treasured memories of my mom making us tea to have with an afternoon snack after school. Anything to do with tea reminds me of my mom. I love brewing sun tea in big glass jars. The square centers of each eight-pointed star remind me of a variety of little tea bags from which to choose!

FINISHED TABLE RUNNER: 14¾" × 37½" | FINISHED BLOCK: 4" × 4"

MATERIALS

Yardage is based on 42"-wide fabric. Fat quarters measure 18" × 21". Fat eighths measure 9" × 21".

- ¼ yard *each* of white dot and white stripe for blocks
- 2 fat eighths of assorted gray prints for blocks
- 2 fat eighths of assorted rose prints for blocks
- 1 fat eighth of aqua floral for blocks
- 1 fat eighth of gray floral for blocks
- 1 fat eighth of white floral for blocks
- 1 fat quarter of aqua print for setting triangles
- ½ yard of rose floral for border and binding
- 1¼ yards of fabric for backing
- 19" × 42" piece of batting

CUTTING

All measurements include ¼" seam allowances.

From *each* of the white dot and white stripe, cut:
4 strips, 1½" × 42"; crosscut into:
    32 rectangles, 1½" × 2½" (64 total)
    32 squares, 1½" × 1½" (64 total)

From *each* of the gray and rose prints, cut:
3 strips, 1½" × 21"; crosscut into 32 squares,
    1½" × 1½" (128 total)

From *each* of the aqua and gray florals, cut:
5 squares, 2½" × 2½" (10 total)

From the white floral, cut:
6 squares, 2½" × 2½"

From the aqua print, cut:
2 squares, 7½" × 7½"; cut into quarters diagonally
    to yield 8 side triangles
2 squares, 7" × 7"; cut in half diagonally to yield
    4 corner triangles

From the rose floral, cut:
3 strips, 2¼" × 42"
3 strips, 2" × 42"; crosscut into:
    2 strips, 2" × 34½"
    2 strips, 2" × 14¾"

MAKING THE BLOCKS

Press all seam allowances in the direction indicated by the arrows.

1 Draw a diagonal line from corner to corner on the wrong side of the gray print and rose print squares. Place a marked gray square on one end of a white dot rectangle, right sides together. Sew on the marked line. Trim the excess corner fabric ¼" from the stitched line. Place a matching gray square on the opposite end of the white dot piece. Sew and trim as before to make a flying-geese unit measuring 1½" × 2½", including seam allowances. Make 32 gray units (16 each of two different gray prints). Repeat using the marked rose squares and white stripe rectangles to make 32 rose units (16 each of two different rose prints).

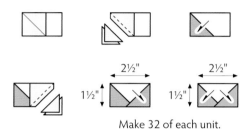

Make 32 of each unit.

2 Lay out four white dot squares, four matching gray flying-geese units, and an aqua, white, or gray floral 2½" square. Sew the squares and units into rows. Join the rows to make a block measuring 4½" square, including seam allowances. Make a total of eight blocks.

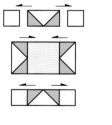

Make 8 blocks,
4½" × 4½".

3 Lay out four white stripe squares, four matching rose flying-geese units, and an aqua, white, or gray floral 2½" square. Sew the squares and units into rows. Join the rows to make a block measuring 4½" square, including seam allowances. Make eight blocks.

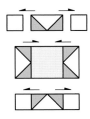

Make 8 blocks,
4½" × 4½".

ASSEMBLING THE TABLE RUNNER

1 Referring to the table-runner assembly diagram, right, arrange and sew the gray blocks and rose blocks together in diagonal rows, adding the aqua side triangles to the ends of each row as indicated. Join the rows, adding the aqua corner triangles last.

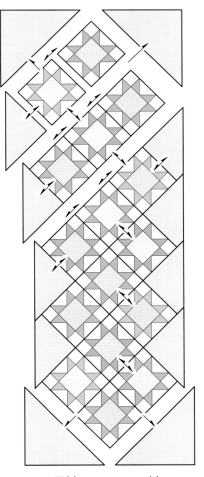

Table-runner assembly

2 Trim and square up the table runner, making sure to leave ¼" beyond the points of all blocks for seam allowances. The table runner should measure 11¾" × 34½", including seam allowances.

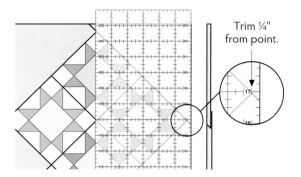

Trim ¼" from point.

3 Sew the rose floral 2" × 34½" strips to the long sides of the runner. Sew the rose floral 2" × 14¾" strips to the ends. The table runner should measure 14¾" × 37½".

FINISHING THE TABLE RUNNER

For more details on any finishing steps, visit ShopMartingale.com/HowtoQuilt for free downloadable information.

1 Layer the runner top with batting and backing; baste the layers together.

2 Quilt by hand or machine. The table runner shown is machine quilted with a floral motif in the blocks. A scroll and loop motif is stitched in the setting triangles and a continuous scroll design is stitched in the border.

3 Use the rose floral 2¼"-wide strips to make double-fold binding. Attach the binding to the table runner.

Family Gathering

There's nothing like gathering around the table with those you love. And often those occasions involve favorite family recipes that have been handed down from generation to generation. The memories around those meals and desserts evoke a shared history that links our lives together. Add to your family traditions with an Irish Chain table topper that's sure to be a crowd-pleaser.

FINISHED TABLE TOPPER: 42½" × 42½" | FINISHED BLOCK: 12" × 12"

MATERIALS

Yardage is based on 42"-wide fabric. Fat eighths measure 9" × 21".

- ¼ yard *each* of 9 assorted light prints for blocks and sashing
- ⅓ yard of green stripe for blocks
- 9 fat eighths of assorted purple prints for blocks and sashing
- ⅜ yard of purple print for binding
- 2¾ yards of fabric for backing
- 49" × 49" piece of batting

CUTTING

All measurements include ¼" seam allowances.

From *each* of the assorted light prints, cut:
2 strips, 2" × 42"; crosscut into:
    4 strips, 2" × 9½" (36 total)
    4 pieces, 2" × 3½" (36 total)

From the remainder of the light prints, cut a *total* of:
24 strips, 2" × 12½"

From the green stripe, cut:
4 strips, 2" × 42"; crosscut into 36 pieces, 2" × 3½"

From *each* of the purple fat eighths, cut:
5 squares, 3½" × 3½" (45 total)
6 squares, 2" × 2" (54 total; 2 are extra)

From the purple print for binding, cut:
5 strips, 2¼" × 42"

MAKING THE BLOCKS

Press all seam allowances in the direction indicated by the arrows.

1 Join a light piece and a green 2" × 3½" piece to make a side unit measuring 3½" square, including seam allowances. Make nine sets of four matching units (36 total).

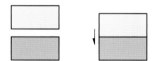

Make 9 sets of 4 matching units,
3½" × 3½".

2 Lay out five matching purple 3½" squares and four matching side units. Sew the squares and units into rows. Join the rows to make a center unit measuring 9½" square, including seam allowances. Make nine units.

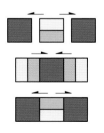

Make 9 units,
9½" × 9½".

3 Lay out four matching light 2" × 9½" strips, four matching purple 2" squares, and one center unit. The light and purple prints should be the same throughout. Sew the pieces into rows. Join the rows to make a block measuring 12½" square, including seam allowances. Make nine blocks.

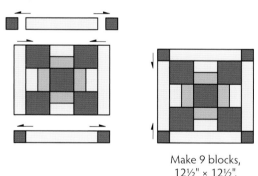

Make 9 blocks,
12½" × 12½".

ASSEMBLING THE TABLE TOPPER

1 Join four purple 2" squares and three light 2" × 12½" strips to make a sashing row. Make four rows measuring 2" × 42½", including seam allowances.

Make 4 sashing rows,
2" × 42½".

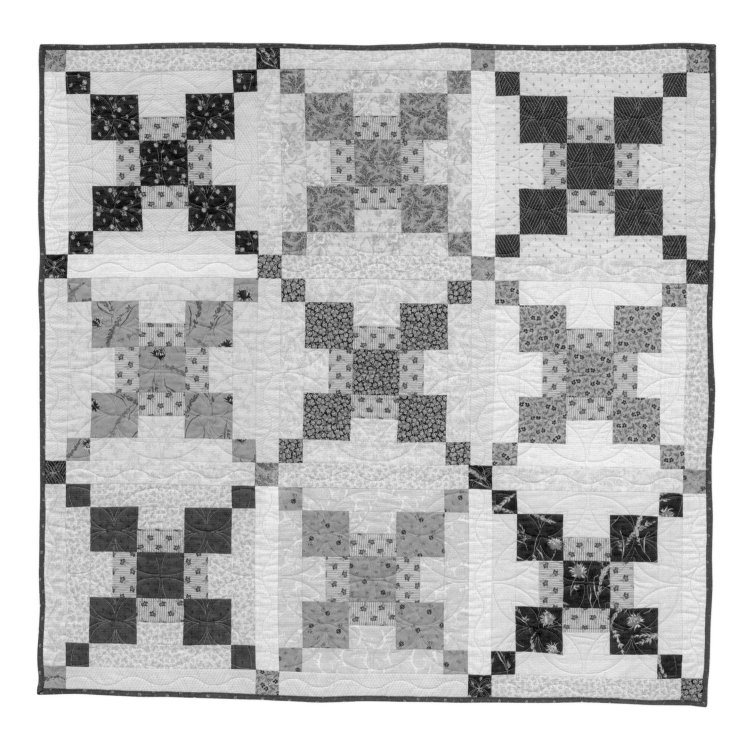

2 Join four light 2" × 12½" strips and three blocks to make a block row. Make three rows measuring 12½" × 42½", including seam allowances.

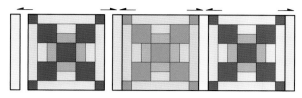

Make 3 block rows,
12½" × 42½".

3 Join the sashing rows and block rows, alternating them as shown in the table-topper assembly diagram below. The table topper should measure 42½" square.

FINISHING THE TABLE TOPPER

For more details on any finishing steps, visit ShopMartingale.com/HowtoQuilt for free downloadable information.

1 Layer the quilt top with batting and backing; baste the layers together.

2 Quilt by hand or machine. The table topper shown is machine quilted with a pumpkin seed design in the blocks. A wavy line is stitched in the sashing.

3 Use the purple 2¼"-wide strips to make double-fold binding. Attach the binding to the table topper.

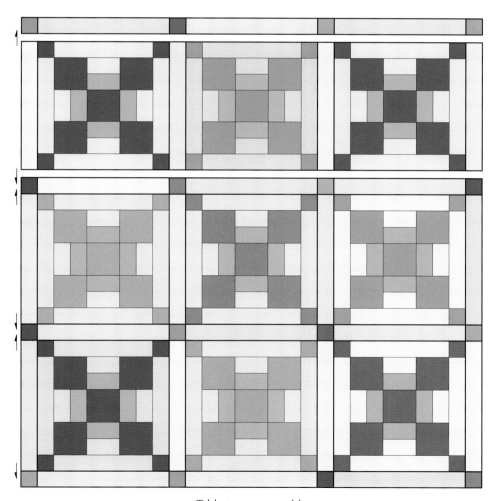

Table-topper assembly

Madge's Apple Cake

SERVES: 10
PREP TIME: 30 MINUTES | BAKING TIME: 60 MINUTES

INGREDIENTS

Apple Cake

- 3 large apples
- 3 cups all-purpose flour
- 2 cups granulated sugar
- 1 cup cooking oil
- 4 eggs
- ½ cup orange-and-pineapple juice (just orange or just pineapple works fine)

- 2½ teaspoons baking powder
- 1 teaspoon salt
- ¼ to ½ cup black walnuts, finely chopped (regular walnuts work)

Cinnamon Topping

- 5 tablespoons granulated sugar
- 2 teaspoons cinnamon

DIRECTIONS

Preheat oven to 350°. Grease well and lightly flour a tube or bundt pan. Pare and slice the apples. In a large bowl, combine all ingredients except the apples and walnuts. Beat until smooth. Stir in walnuts. Pour half of the batter into the pan. Arrange half of the apples on top. Mix together the sugar and cinnamon and sprinkle half over apples. Pour in remaining batter. Arrange the remaining apples on top and sprinkle the rest of the sugar and cinnamon over them. Bake for 60 minutes or until a toothpick inserted in center comes out clean.

Winter Bliss

When I was a teenager my family lived in Belgium, and each winter we'd go skiing in Austria. After dinner, everyone would gather to tell tales of the ski slopes and swap travel stories. As an adult, my favorite drink at the slopes (or the holidays) is warm Glühwein, which is a mulled red wine with sugar, cloves, and oranges.

FINISHED TABLE TOPPER: 51½" × 51½" | FINISHED BLOCK: 8" × 8"

MATERIALS

Yardage is based on 42"-wide fabric. Fat quarters measure 18" × 21". When choosing fabrics, the A prints in each color should be the darkest value and the C prints in each color should be the lightest value.

- ¾ yard of light print A for blocks and border
- ½ yard of light print B for blocks
- 1 fat quarter *each* of light prints C and D for blocks
- ½ yard *each* of 2 green print A and 2 red print A for blocks
- ¼ yard *each* of 2 green print B and 2 red print B for blocks
- 1 fat quarter *each* of green print C and red print C for blocks
- ½ yard of green print D for binding
- 3¼ yards of fabric for backing
- 58" × 58" piece of batting

CUTTING

All measurements include ¼" seam allowances.

From the light print A, cut:
3 strips, 2½" × 42"; crosscut into 44 squares, 2½" × 2½"
6 strips, 2" × 42"
2 squares, 3" × 3"

From the light print B, cut:
4 strips, 2½" × 42"; crosscut into 56 squares, 2½" × 2½"
4 squares, 3" × 3"

From *each* of the light prints C and D, cut:
12 squares, 2½" × 2½" (24 total)
2 squares, 3" × 3" (4 total)

From *each* of the 2 green A and 2 red A prints, cut:
2 strips, 4½" × 42"; crosscut into:
    10 squares, 4½" × 4½" (40 total)
    2 squares, 3" × 3" (8 total; 1 green and 1 red square are extra)
2 strips, 2½" × 42"; crosscut into 20 squares, 2½" × 2½" (80 total)

Continued on page 52

Continued from page 51

From *each* of the 2 green B and 2 red B prints, cut:

1 strip, 4½" × 42"; crosscut into:
    6 squares, 4½" × 4½" (24 total)
    1 square, 3" × 3" (4 total)
1 strip, 2½" × 42"; crosscut into 12 squares,
    2½" × 2½" (48 total)

From *each* of the green C and red C prints, cut:

4 squares, 4½" × 4½" (8 total)
8 squares, 2½" × 2½" (16 total)

From the green print D, cut:

6 strips, 2¼" × 42"

MAKING THE A, B, AND C BLOCKS

Press all seam allowances in the direction indicated by the arrows.

1 To make block A, lay out two green A, two red A, and four light A 2½" squares. Join the squares to make two small four patches. Lay out a red A and a green A 4½" square with the small four patches. Join the pieces to make block A measuring 8½" square, including seam allowances. Make eight blocks.

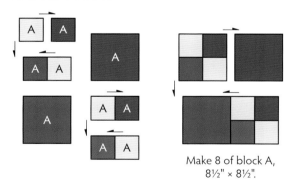

Make 8 of block A,
8½" × 8½".

2 To make block B, lay out two green B, two green A, and four light B 2½" squares. Join the squares to make two small four patches. Lay out a green B 4½" and a green A 4½" square with the small four patches. Join the pieces to make block B

measuring 8½" square, including seam allowances. Make four blocks.

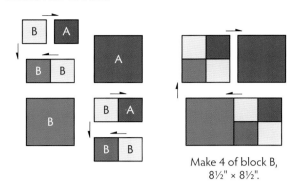

Make 4 of block B,
8½" × 8½".

3 To make block C, lay out two red A, two red B, and four light B 2½" squares. Join the squares to make two small four patches. Lay out a red A and a red B 4½" square with the small four patches. Join the pieces to make block C measuring 8½" square, including seam allowances. Make four blocks.

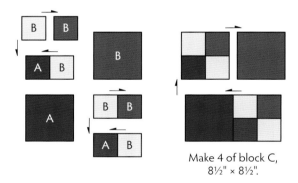

Make 4 of block C,
8½" × 8½".

MAKING THE D–M BLOCKS

1 Draw a diagonal line from corner to corner on the wrong side of each light A–D 3" square. Place a marked C square right sides together with a green B 3" square. Sew ¼" from both sides of the drawn line. Cut the unit apart on the marked line to make two half-square-triangle units. Make four units and trim them to measure 2½" square, including seam allowances.

Make 4 B/C units.

2 Using the marked squares and the green and red 3" squares, repeat step 1 to make the number of units in the colors indicated below.

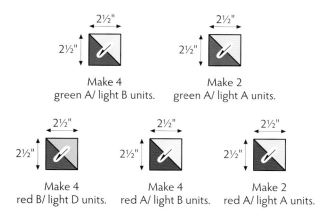

Make 4
green A/ light B units.

Make 2
green A/ light A units.

Make 4
red B/ light D units.

Make 4
red A/ light B units.

Make 2
red A/ light A units.

3 To make block D, lay out two green C, two green B, and three light C 2½" squares along with a green B and a green C 4½" square and a green B/C triangle unit. Make four patches; join the four patches and large squares to make two rows. Join the rows to make a block measuring 8½" square, including seam allowances. Make two of block D. Repeat to make two of block E, reversing the orientation of the pieces.

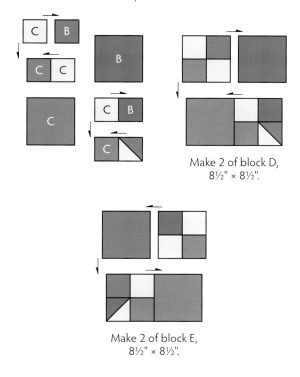

Make 2 of block D,
8½" × 8½".

Make 2 of block E,
8½" × 8½".

4 To make block F, lay out one A/B half-square triangle unit, two green A, two green B, and three light B 2½" squares. Join the pieces to make two small four patches. Lay out one green A and one green B 4½" square with the small four patches. Join the pieces to make block F measuring 8½" square, including seam allowances. Make two of block F. Repeat to make two of block G, reversing the orientation of the pieces.

5 To make block H, lay out one red B/light D half-square triangle unit, two red B, two red C, and three light D 2½" squares. Join the pieces to make two small four patches. Lay out one red C and one red B 4½" square with the small four patches. Join the pieces to make block H measuring 8½" square, including seam allowances. Make two of block H. Repeat to make two of block I, reversing the orientation of the pieces.

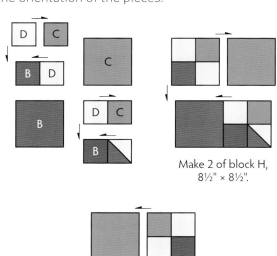

Make 2 of block F,
8½" × 8½".

Make 2 of block H,
8½" × 8½".

Make 2 of block G,
8½" × 8½".

Make 2 of block I,
8½" × 8½".

6 To make block J, lay out one A/B half-square triangle unit, two red A, two red B, and three light B 2½" squares. Join the pieces to make two small four patches. Lay out one red A and one red B 4½" square with the small four patches. Join the pieces to make block J measuring 8½" square, including seam allowances. Make two of block J. Repeat to make two of block K, reversing the orientation of the pieces.

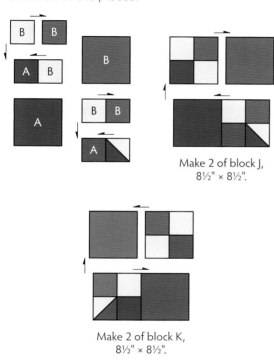

Make 2 of block J,
8½" × 8½".

Make 2 of block K,
8½" × 8½".

7 To make block L, lay out one green A/A half-square triangle unit, two green A, two red A, and three light A 2½" squares. Join the pieces to make two small four patches. Lay out one green A and one red A 4½" square with the small four patches. Join the pieces to make block L measuring 8½" square, including seam allowances. Make two

of block L. Repeat to make two of block M, reversing the orientation of the squares and using a red A/A triangle unit.

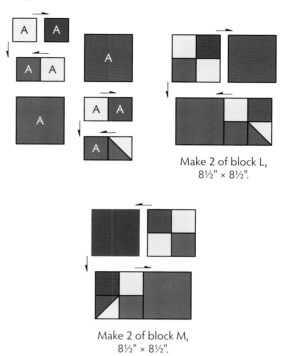

Make 2 of block L,
8½" × 8½".

Make 2 of block M,
8½" × 8½".

ASSEMBLING THE TABLE TOPPER

1 Lay out two of block A and one of blocks B, C, D, F, H, J, and L in three rows of three blocks each. Sew the blocks into rows. Join the rows to make a quadrant measuring 24½" square, including seam allowances. Make two quadrants.

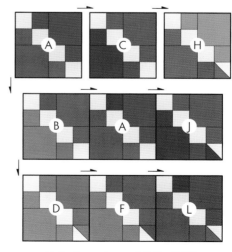

Make 2 quadrants, 24½" × 24½".

2 Lay out two of block A and one of blocks B, C, E, G, I, K, and M in three rows of three blocks each. Sew the blocks into rows. Join the rows to make a quadrant measuring 24½" square, including seam allowances. Make two quadrants.

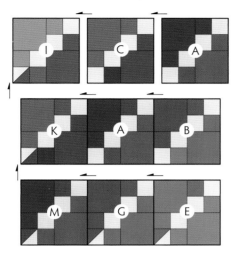

Make 2 quadrants, 24½" × 24½".

3 Referring to the table-topper assembly diagram at right, lay out the quadrants from steps 1 and 2, rotating the quadrants in the bottom row to form a pinwheel in the center of the table topper. Sew the quadrants into rows. Join the rows. The topper should measure 48½" square, including seam allowances.

Portable Design Wall

No design wall? Try this trick: Use an inexpensive, flannel-backed vinyl tablecloth. Roll it out (flannel-side up) and position your blocks on the flannel. If you have to pause midway through construction, simply roll up the tablecloth with the blocks inside still in position. The next chance you have to sew, you'll be all set!

4 Join the light A 2"-wide strips end to end. From the pieced strip, cut two 51½"-long strips and two 48½"-long strips. Sew the shorter strips to the left and right sides of the topper. Sew the longer strips to the top and bottom edges. The table topper should measure 51½" square.

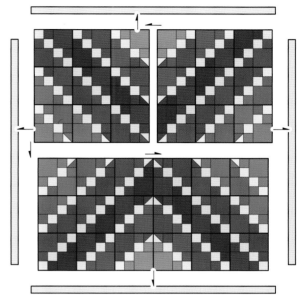

Table-topper assembly

FINISHING THE TABLE TOPPER

For more details on any finishing steps, visit ShopMartingale.com/HowtoQuilt for free downloadable information.

1 Layer the topper top with batting and backing; baste the layers together.

2 Quilt by hand or machine. The table topper shown is machine quilted with a continuous fern design in the red and green areas. A single leaf motif is stitched in the light squares and border.

3 Use the green D 2¼"-wide strips to make double-fold binding. Attach the binding to the table topper.

French Bistro

There's nothing better than a perfect French croissant—a taste of heaven! In my neighborhood, a new French bistro opened; they sell yummy coffees, cakes, and, yes, croissants. The layer upon delicious layer of buttery goodness reminds me of these layers of skinny strips in favorite prints. Indulge in an authentic croissant and your fabric faves!

FINISHED TABLE RUNNER: 20" × 48½" | FINISHED BLOCK: 12" × 12"

MATERIALS

Yardage is based on 42"-wide fabric. Fat eighths measure 9" × 21".

- 16 fat eighths of assorted prints *OR* assorted 1½"-wide strips for blocks
- ¼ yard of navy solid for blocks and inner border
- ⅝ yard of aqua floral for outer border and binding
- 1½ yards of fabric for backing
- 24" × 53" piece of batting

CUTTING

All measurements include ¼" seam allowances.

From *each* of the assorted prints, cut:
2 strips, 1½" × 21"; crosscut into 6 strips, 1½" × 6½" (96 total)

From the navy solid, cut:
1 strip, 2½" × 42"; crosscut into 8 squares, 2½" × 2½"
3 strips, 1¼" × 42"

From the aqua floral, cut:
3 strips, 3½" × 42"
4 strips, 2¼" × 42"

MAKING THE BLOCKS

Press all seam allowances in the direction indicated by the arrows.

1 Join six different 1½" × 6½" strips to make a strip unit measuring 6½" square, including seam allowances. Make 16 units.

Make 16 units, 6½" × 6½".

2 Draw a diagonal line from corner to corner on the wrong side of the navy squares. Place a marked square on one corner of a strip unit, right sides together. Sew on the marked line. Trim the excess corner fabric ¼" from the stitched line. Make eight units measuring 6½" square, including seam allowances.

3 Lay out two units from step 1 and two units from step 2, rotating the units so that the triangles are in the center. Sew the units into rows. Join the rows to make a block measuring 12½" square, including seam allowances. Make four blocks.

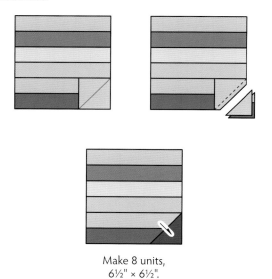

Make 8 units,
6½" × 6½".

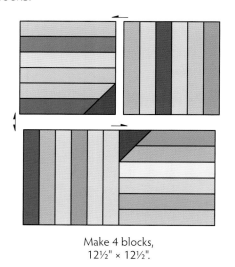

Make 4 blocks,
12½" × 12½".

ASSEMBLING THE TABLE RUNNER

1 Join the blocks to make the table-runner center measuring 12½" × 48½", including seam allowances.

2 Join the navy 1¼"-wide strips end to end. From the pieced strip, cut two 48½"-long strips. Sew the strips to the long sides of the runner. The table runner should measure 14" × 48½", including seam allowances.

3 Join the aqua 3½"-wide strips end to end. From the pieced strip, cut two 48½"-long strips. Sew the strips to the long sides of the runner. The table runner should measure 20" × 48½".

FINISHING THE TABLE RUNNER

For more details on any finishing steps, visit ShopMartingale.com/HowtoQuilt for free downloadable information.

1 Layer the runner top with batting and backing; baste the layers together.

2 Quilt by hand or machine. The table runner shown is machine quilted with variegated thread in an allover ogee design.

3 Use the aqua floral 2¼"-wide strips to make double-fold binding. Attach the binding to the table runner.

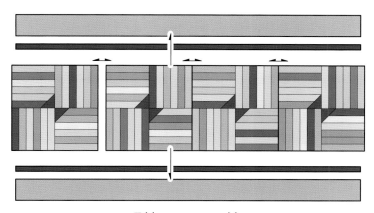

Table-runner assembly

U-Pick

Whether it was fresh berries and cherries by the basket or apples by the bushel, we'd eat our fill as kids on the way home from the fields. And no outing was complete until baked goods that incorporated the fruits from our labor were served. Pulling fabrics for a project has a u-pick fun feel as well, when choices yield delicious results!

FINISHED TABLE TOPPER: 45½" × 45½" | FINISHED BLOCK: 12" × 12"

MATERIALS

Yardage is based on 42"-wide fabric. Fat quarters measure 18" × 21". Fat eighths measure 9" × 21".

- 6 fat quarters of assorted black prints for blocks and pieced border
- 4 fat quarters of assorted blue prints for blocks and pieced border
- 2 fat quarters of assorted gold prints for blocks and pieced border
- 2 fat quarters of assorted orange prints for blocks and pieced border
- ½ yard of black-and-white polka dot for blocks and inner border
- 6 fat eighths of assorted light prints for blocks
- ⅜ yard of black print for binding
- 3 yards of fabric for backing
- 52" × 52" piece of batting

CUTTING

As you cut, keep like fabrics together. All measurements include ¼" seam allowances.

From *each* of the black print fat quarters, cut:
3 pieces, 3½" × 5" (18 total)
3 pieces, 2" × 3½" (18 total)

From *each of 3* black print fat quarters, cut:
12 pieces, 2" × 3½" (36 total)

From *1* black print fat quarter, cut:
4 squares, 3½" × 3½"

From *1* of the blue prints, cut:
3 pieces, 3½" × 5"
3 pieces, 2" × 3½"

From *each* of the remaining blue prints, cut:
2 pieces, 3½" × 5" (6 total)
2 pieces, 2" × 3½" (6 total)

From *1* of the gold prints, cut:
3 pieces, 3½" × 5"
3 pieces, 2" × 3½"

Continued on page 64

Continued from page 63

From the remaining gold print, cut:

2 pieces, 3½" × 5"

2 pieces, 2" × 3½"

From *each* of the orange prints, cut:

2 pieces, 3½" × 5" (4 total)

2 pieces, 2" × 3½" (4 total)

From *each* of 2 blue, 2 gold, and 2 orange prints, cut:

12 pieces, 2" × 3½" (72 total; 4 are extra)

From the black-and-white polka dot, cut:

2 strips, 3½" × 42"; crosscut into:

    7 squares, 3½" × 3½"

    14 pieces, 2" × 3½"

4 strips, 2" × 42"; crosscut into:

    2 strips, 2" × 39½"

    2 strips, 2" × 36½"

From *each* of the assorted light prints, cut:

5 squares, 3½" × 3½" (30 total; 1 is extra)

10 pieces, 2" × 3½" (60 total; 2 are extra)

From the black print for binding, cut:

5 strips, 2¼" × 42"

MAKING THE BLOCKS

For *each* quarter-block unit, you'll need one square and two pieces from one light print or the polka dot. You'll also need one 2" × 3½" and one 3½" × 5" piece from one black, blue, gold, or orange print. Press all seam allowances in the direction indicated by the arrows.

1   Sew a light or polka dot piece to a black, blue, gold, or orange 2" × 3½" piece to make a unit measuring 3½" square, including seam allowances. Make 36 units.

Make 36 units,
3½" × 3½".

2   Using the same fabrics you used in step 1, sew a light or polka dot piece to a black, blue, gold, or orange 3½" × 5" piece to make a unit measuring 3½" × 6½", including seam allowances. Make 36 units.

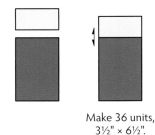

Make 36 units,
3½" × 6½".

3   Sew a matching light or polka dot square to the top of a unit from step 1. Sew a matching unit from step 2 to the right edge to make a quarter-block unit. Make 36 units measuring 6½" square, including seam allowances.

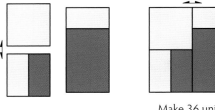

Make 36 units,
6½" × 6½".

4   Lay out two different black units and two different blue, gold, or orange units. Sew the units into rows. Join the rows to make a block measuring 12½" square, including seam allowances. Make eight blocks.

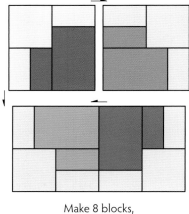

Make 8 blocks,
12½" × 12½".

A Word About Words

When making a table topper, I don't worry about which direction text prints will run. Because the table topper will likely be viewed from all directions around the table, I see no reason to fret over text print placement as I sew the fabrics into the finished piece!

5 Sew a black unit to a blue, gold, or orange unit to make a half block measuring 6½" × 12½", including seam allowances. Make two half blocks.

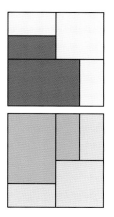 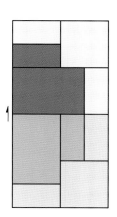

Make 2 half blocks,
6½" × 12½".

ASSEMBLING THE TABLE TOPPER

Refer to the photo on page 66 for color placement guidance as needed.

1 Referring to the table-topper assembly diagram on page 67, join three blocks to make the top row, which should measure 12½" × 36½", including seam allowances. Repeat to make the bottom row.

2 Join the two half-blocks and the remaining two blocks to make the center row, which should measure 12½" × 36½", including seam allowances.

3 Join the rows to make the table-topper center, which should measure 36½" square, including seam allowances.

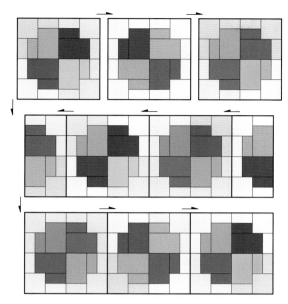

Table-topper assembly

4 Sew the polka dot 2" × 36½" strips to the top and bottom edges of the table topper. Sew the polka dot 2" × 39½" strips to the left and right sides. The table topper should measure 39½" square, including seam allowances.

5 Join 26 black, blue, gold, and orange 2" × 3½" pieces, alternating them as shown, to make the top border which should measure 3½" × 39½", including seam allowances. Repeat to make the bottom border. Make two more borders in the same way, adding a black 3½" square to each end. The side borders should measure 3½" × 45½", including seam allowances.

Make 2 side borders,
3½" × 39½".

Make 2 top/bottom borders,
3½" × 45½".

6 Sew the shorter borders to the top and bottom edges of the table topper and then sew the longer borders to the left and right sides. The table topper should measure 45½" square.

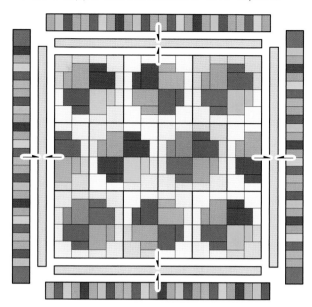

Adding the borders

FINISHING THE TABLE TOPPER

For more details on any finishing steps, visit ShopMartingale.com/HowtoQuilt for free downloadable information.

1 Layer the topper top with batting and backing; baste the layers together.

2 Quilt by hand or machine. The table topper shown is machine quilted with evenly spaced wavy lines from top to bottom.

3 Use the black 2¼"-wide strips to make double-fold binding. Attach the binding to the table topper.

Breakfast Club

It's fun to get together with your special someone(s) over a cup of coffee or tea and enjoy a delicious pastry. Mornings are often too busy for a slow start, but I think that's what makes moments when we can savor our time together even more special. A solo star bursting forth from the center is like my heart on days like these!

FINISHED TABLE TOPPER: 34½" × 34½" | FINISHED BLOCK: 24" × 24"

MATERIALS

Yardage is based on 42"-wide fabric. Fat quarters measure 18" × 21".

- 1 fat quarter of white print for block
- ½ yard of green print for block and binding
- 2 fat quarters of red prints A and B for blocks
- ⅝ yard of white dot for block and inner border
- ½ yard of red print C for outer border
- 1⅛ yards of fabric for backing
- 39" × 39" piece of batting

CUTTING

All measurements include ¼" seam allowances.

From the white print, cut:
1 square, 6½" × 6½"
4 squares, 4" × 4"

From the green print, cut:
1 strip, 4" × 42"; crosscut into 8 squares, 4" × 4"
1 strip, 3½" × 42"; crosscut into 4 squares, 3½" × 3½"
4 strips, 2¼" × 42"

From *each* of red prints A and B, cut:
6 squares, 4" × 4" (12 total)
6 squares, 3½" × 3½" (12 total)

From the white dot, cut:
1 strip, 4" × 42"; crosscut into:
    8 squares, 4" × 4"
    1 square, 3½" × 3½"
1 strip, 3½" × 42"; crosscut into 11 squares, 3½" × 3½"
4 strips, 2½" × 42"; crosscut into:
    2 strips, 2½" × 28½"
    2 strips, 2½" × 24½"

From the red print C, cut:
4 strips, 3½" × 42"; crosscut into:
    2 strips, 3½" × 34½"
    2 strips, 3½" × 28½"

MAKING THE CENTER STAR

Press all seam allowances in the direction indicated by the arrows.

1 Draw a diagonal line from corner to corner on the wrong side of each white print 4" square. Place a marked square right sides together with a green 4" square. Sew ¼" from both sides of the drawn line. Cut the unit apart on the marked line to make two half-square-triangle units. Make eight units and trim them to measure 3½" square, including seam allowances.

Make 8 units.

2 Join two half-square-triangle units from step 1 to make a side unit measuring 3½" × 6½", including seam allowances. Make four units.

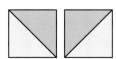 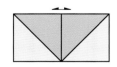

Make 4 units, 3½" × 6½".

3 Lay out four green 3½" squares, four side units, and one white print 6½" square. Sew the squares and units into rows. Join the rows to make the center star measuring 12½" square, including seam allowances.

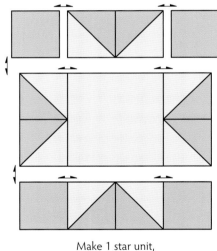

Make 1 star unit, 12½" × 12½".

MAKING THE BLOCK

1 Draw a diagonal line from corner to corner on the wrong side of the remaining green and the white dot 4" squares. Place a marked green square right sides together with a red A 4" square. Sew ¼" from both sides of the drawn line. Cut the unit apart on the marked line to make two half-square-triangle units. Make four units and trim them to measure 3½" square, including seam allowances. In the same way, make eight units using the marked white dot squares and remaining red A 4" squares.

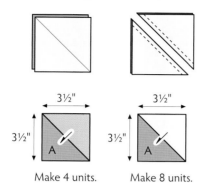

Make 4 units.   Make 8 units.

2 Use the remaining marked green and white dot squares and the red B 4" squares to make four green/red B units and eight white/red B units.

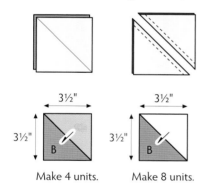

Make 4 units.   Make 8 units.

3 Lay out one green/red A triangle unit, one red B 3½" square, one red A 3½" square, and one green/red B triangle unit. Join the pieces to make a unit measuring 3½" × 12½", including seam allowances. Make four side units.

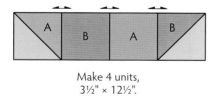

Make 4 units,
3½" × 12½".

4 Lay out two red A 3½" squares, two red B 3½" squares, the side units from step 3, and the center star. Sew the pieces into rows. Join the rows to make a unit measuring 18½" square, including seam allowances.

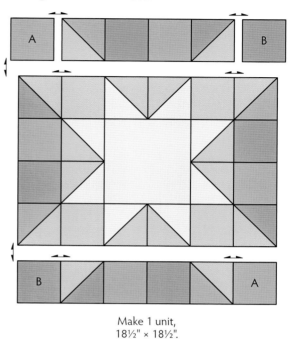

Make 1 unit,
18½" × 18½".

5 Lay out two white dot 3½" squares, two white/red B triangle units, and two white/red A triangle units. Join the pieces to make a unit measuring 3½" × 18½", including seam allowances. Make two top and bottom units and two side units.

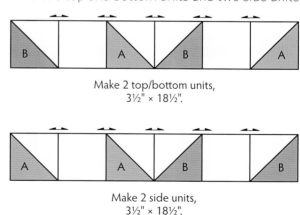

Make 2 top/bottom units,
3½" × 18½".

Make 2 side units,
3½" × 18½".

6 Lay out four white dot 3½" squares, the units from step 5, and the unit from step 4. Sew the pieces into rows. Join the rows to make a block measuring 24½" square, including seam allowances.

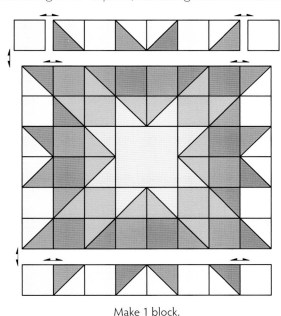

Make 1 block,
24½" × 24½".

ASSEMBLING THE TABLE TOPPER

1 Sew the white dot 2½" × 24½" strips to the left and right sides of the block. Sew the white dot 2½" × 28½" strips to the top and bottom edges. The table topper should measure 28½" square, including seam allowances.

2 Sew the red C 3½" × 28½" strips to the left and right sides of the block. Sew the red C 3½" × 34½" strips to the top and bottom edges. The table topper should measure 34½" square.

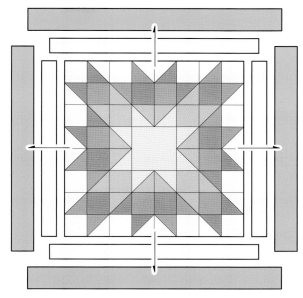

Table-topper assembly

FINISHING THE TABLE TOPPER

For more details on any finishing steps, visit ShopMartingale.com/HowtoQuilt for free downloadable information.

1 Layer the topper top with batting and backing; baste the layers together.

2 Quilt by hand or machine. The table topper shown is machine quilted with a sunburst design of circles, squiggly lines, and swirls. Swirls are stitched in the inner border and a flower motif is stitched in the outer border.

3 Use the green 2¼"-wide strips to make double-fold binding. Attach the binding to the table topper.

Summer Fun

I'm not much for the summer heat, but I will take the longer days and starry nights with friends gathering on the lawn or patio for fun and games. Friendship stars and a friendly little fusible bluebird perfectly portray the best of summer to me. Stir up a pitcher of fresh-squeezed lemonade and you've got it made in the shade!

FINISHED TABLE RUNNER: 18½" × 46½" | FINISHED BLOCK: 9" × 9"

MATERIALS

Yardage is based on 42"-wide fabric.

- ¾ yard of white print for blocks and appliquéd background
- ⅓ yard of navy floral for blocks and bird wings
- ¼ yard of blue print A for blocks and berries
- ¼ yard of blue print B for blocks, bird tail, and inner border
- ½ yard of blue stripe for vines and binding
- 10" × 10" square of blue print C for bird bodies
- Scraps of navy print for bird beaks and eyes
- 1½ yards of fabric for backing
- 25" × 53" piece of batting
- ¼ yard of paper-backed fusible web
- ½" bias-tape maker
- 50-weight thread in colors to match appliqués

CUTTING

All measurements include ¼" seam allowances.

From the white print, cut:
1 strip, 4½" × 42"; crosscut into 2 strips, 4½" × 18½"
2 strips, 4" × 42"; crosscut into 16 squares, 4" × 4"
2 strips, 3½" × 42"; crosscut into 16 squares, 3½" × 3½"
2 strips, 2" × 42"

From the navy floral, cut:
2 strips, 4" × 42"; crosscut into 16 squares, 4" × 4"

From the blue print A, cut:
2 strips, 2" × 42"

From the blue print B, cut:
1 strip, 3½" × 42"; crosscut into 8 squares, 3½" × 3½"
1 strip, 1½" × 42"; crosscut into 2 strips, 1½" × 18½"

From the blue stripe, cut:
4 strips, 2¼" × 42"
1"-wide strips cut on the bias to total 48"

MAKING THE BLOCKS

Press all seam allowances in the direction indicated by the arrows.

1 Draw a diagonal line from corner to corner on the wrong side of each white 4" square. Place a marked square right sides together with a navy floral 4" square. Sew ¼" from both sides of the drawn line. Cut the unit apart on the marked line to make two half-square-triangle units. Make 32 units and trim them to measure 3½" square, including seam allowances.

Make 32 units.

2 Sew a white 2"-wide strip to the long side of a blue A strip to make a strip set measuring 3½" × 42", including seam allowances. Make two strip sets. Cut the strip sets into 32 segments, 2" × 3½".

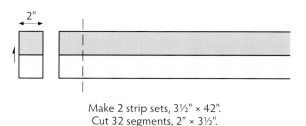

Make 2 strip sets, 3½" × 42".
Cut 32 segments, 2" × 3½".

3 Join two segments from step 2 to make a four-patch unit as shown. Make 16 units measuring 3½" square, including seam allowances.

Make 16 units,
3½" × 3½".

4 Lay out two white 3½" squares, four half-square-triangle units, two four-patch units, and one blue B square. Sew the pieces into rows. Join the rows to make a block measuring 9½" square, including seam allowances. Make eight blocks.

ASSEMBLING THE TABLE RUNNER

Lay out the blocks in two rows of four blocks each, rotating the blocks as shown in the table-runner assembly diagram. Sew the blocks into rows. Join the rows to make the table runner, which should measure 18½" × 36½", including seam allowances.

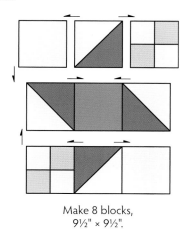

Make 8 blocks,
9½" × 9½".

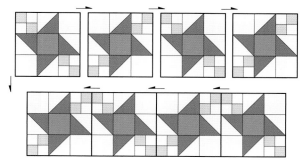

Table-runner assembly

ADDING THE BORDERS

1 To make the vines, place one end of the blue stripe 1"-wide bias strip into a ½" bias-tape maker. Pull just the tip of the strip through the bias-tape maker. Continue to pull the bias-tape maker slowly along the strip, pressing the strip with your iron to crease the edges of the fabric as it emerges from the bias-tape maker. Cut the long strip into two ½" × 24" vines.

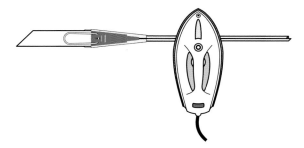

2 Using the patterns on page 79, trace each shape the number of times indicated onto the fusible web. Roughly cut out each shape, about ½" beyond the drawn line. For larger shapes, such as the bird body, cut through the excess web around the shape, through the marked line, and into the interior of the shape. Cut away the excess fusible web on the inside of the shape, leaving about ¼" inside the drawn line.

3 Position the fusible-web shapes on the fabrics indicated on the patterns. Fuse as instructed

by the manufacturer. Cut out the shapes on the marked line and remove the paper backing from each shape.

4 Referring to the appliqué placement diagram, position one vine, then position the prepared appliqué shapes on a white 4½" × 18½" strip. Repeat to make a second border.

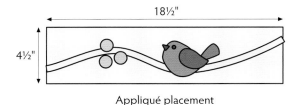

Appliqué placement

5 Fuse the appliqués in place. Blanket-stitch around the outer edge of each shape using matching thread.

A Point to Remember

For smoother stitching when you're machine blanket stitching around the outside curves of the body and wing, stop with the needle down in the fabric on the right-hand swing of the needle. Lift the presser foot, pivot the appliqué foundation slightly, lower the presser foot, and continue sewing.

---

6 Sew a blue B 1½" × 18½" strip to the top of each appliquéd border. The border should measure 5½" × 18½", including seam allowances.

7 Sew a border to each end of the table runner so it measures 18½" × 46½".

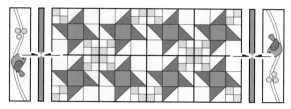

Adding the borders

FINISHING THE TABLE RUNNER

For more details on any finishing steps, visit ShopMartingale.com/HowtoQuilt for free downloadable information.

1 Layer the runner top with batting and backing; baste the layers together.

2 Quilt by hand or machine. The table runner shown is machine quilted in the ditch around the stars and appliqués. Straight lines are stitched diagonally across the blocks. A meandering motif is stitched in the background.

3 Use the blue stripe 2¼"-wide strips to make double-fold binding. Attach the binding to the table runner.

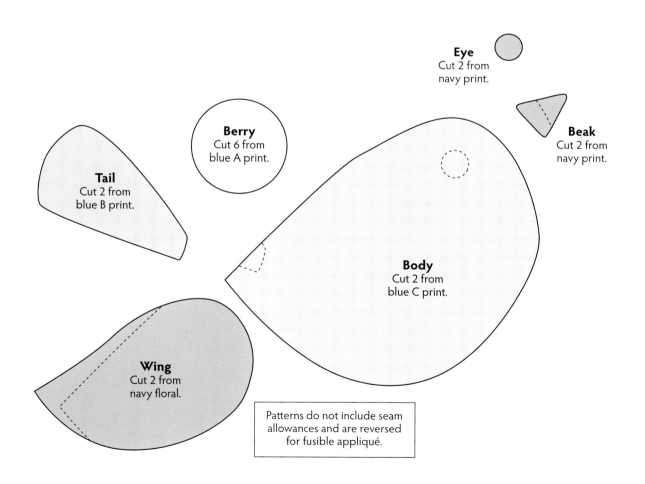

Eye
Cut 2 from navy print.

Berry
Cut 6 from blue A print.

Beak
Cut 2 from navy print.

Tail
Cut 2 from blue B print.

Body
Cut 2 from blue C print.

Wing
Cut 2 from navy floral.

Patterns do not include seam allowances and are reversed for fusible appliqué.

Acknowledgments

Many thanks to my friends for helping make this book come true: Cindy and Dennis Dickinson, Melanie Barrett, and Judy Clark. A huge thank you to my wonderful business partners: Aurifil (thread), Benartex (fabric), Fat Quarter Shop, Oliso (iron), OLFA (cutters), and my wonderful Baby Lock sewing-machine family. And thank you to my editor, Nancy Mahoney, and my wonderful publisher, Martingale.

About the Author

I'm a quilt designer, author, teacher, YouTuber, and fabric designer. My passion is to make quilting fun for everyone. I love to make quilts, share quilts, and talk about quilts. I host a very active, friendly, and exciting quilting community on Facebook called Quilt Along with Pat Sloan. I host lots of sew-alongs and challenges, and we have so much fun—please join us! Find me at PatSloan.com and sign up for my notices. I can't wait to chat with you!